Lots of Bugs

Written by Michèle Dufresne

PIONEER VALLEY EDUCATIONAL PRESS, INC.

Look at the bug.
The bug can sit
in the sun.

Insects play an important
part in pollinating plants.
Insects carry the pollen
from flower to flower.

Look at the bug.
Is it a big bug?
Yes! It is a big,
big **beetle**.

Many beetles live in the rain forest. The world's longest beetle is the Hercules beetle. It can be more than 7 inches long.

Look at the **fly**.
A fly is a bug.
Bugs have six legs.

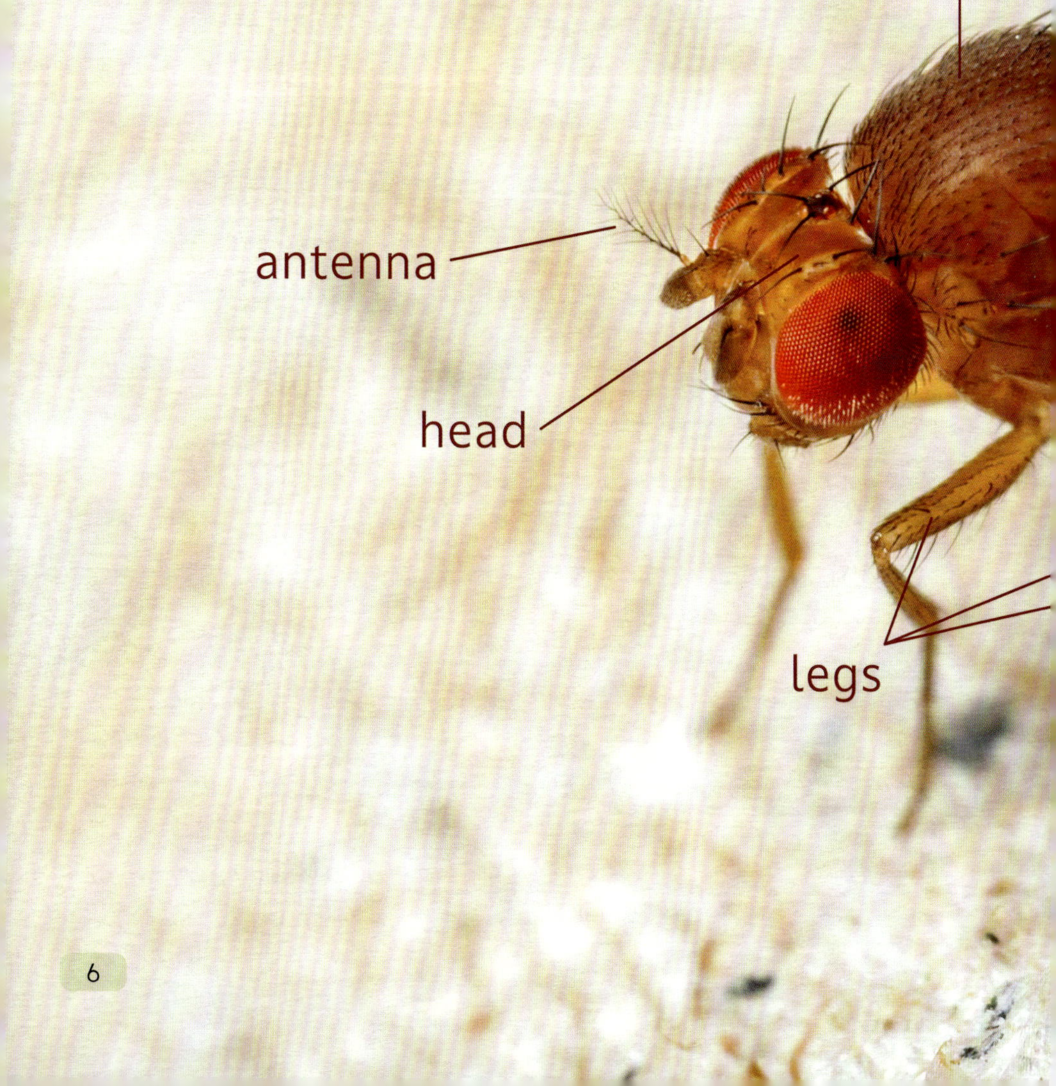

thorax

antenna

head

legs

wings
abdomen

Here is a **spider**.

A spider is not a bug.

Spiders are not insects.

Spiders have eight legs.

Look at the bug.

It is an **ant**.

The ant can dig.

Ants dig tunnels that can reach as deep as 25 feet below ground.

glossary

beetle

fly

spider

ant